US

FRIENDS
OF ACPL

D1037364

CB Radio

By Edward Radlauer

AN ELK GROVE BOOK

 CHILDRENS PRESS, CHICAGO

Created by Radlauer Productions, Inc. for Childrens Press.

The author thanks Barbara Mellman
of Pathcom, Incorporated for help
with the photography.

Photo Credits: Pathcom, Inc., pages 4 and 13

Library of Congress Cataloging in Publication Data
Radlauer, Edward.
        CB radio.
        ''An Elk Grove book.''
        Includes index.
        SUMMARY: Briefly explains how Citizen Band Radio
works and translates the special language of CBers.
        1. Citizens band radio—Juvenile literature.
[1. Citizens band radio] I. Title.
TK6570.C5R26   384.5'3   77-20064
ISBN 0-516-07468-7

Copyright © 1978 by Regensteiner Publishing Enterprises, Inc.
All rights reserved. Published simultaneously in Canada.
Printed in the United States of America.

1 2 3 4 5 6 7 8 9 10 11 12 13 14 15 R 84 83 82 81 80 79 78

Ready, Get Set, Go Books

Ready

Motorcycle Mania
Flying Mania
Skateboard Mania
Shark Mania
Monkey Mania

Get Set

Fast, Faster, Fastest
Wild Wheels
Racing Numbers
Boats
CB Radio

Go

Soap Box Racing
Ready, Get Set, Whoa!
Model Airplanes
Model Cars
Soccer

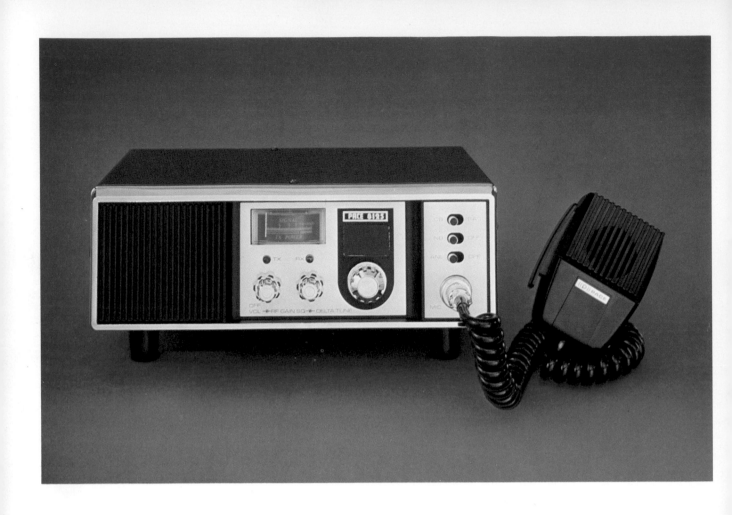

CB radios. People say they're handy.
They're handy when you want to call a friend.
And they're handy when you need help.

CB — Citizen band

U. S. 1998276

      CB is short for Citizen Band.
Citizens are people. Band is a word that
tells what kind of signals a radio can send
or receive. To hear or talk to someone else,
your radio must be on the same band as the
other person's radio. Citizens or **CBers**
using the same band can talk to each other.
They can say things like, ''Meet me at the
eatem up,'' or ''I'm **on the peg**.''

CBer — person using CB radio
eatem up — restaurant
on the peg — going the speed limit

5

Your CB radio needs an antenna.
The antenna sends out radio waves of what
you say when you're in the cab of your big
Fruitliner. It also picks up radio waves
from other **good buddies**.

Fruitliner — White Freightliner truck
good buddies — other CBers

6

Radio waves travel through the air.
If CB radios are too powerful, the radio
waves will go too far. If that happens, all the
good buddies' **shouts** will get **walked on**.
So most of your **jaw jacking** will be through
the **ears** of some nearby good buddies.

shout — call on the radio
walked on — CB message spoiled by another CB radio
jaw jacking — talking
ears — a CB radio

Use the microphone to start jaw jacking with another good buddy. Your voice goes from the microphone into the CB set. The set changes your voice into radio waves that go out the **scatter stick**. Hold the microphone in your hand and say, "**Breaker**, breaker, anyone have ears?"

scatter stick — antenna
breaker — I want to talk

8

Most CB **mikes** have a push-to-talk button. Pushing the button on the mike turns on the sending part of your **rig**. Leave the button out and your radio receives what other CBers say into their mikes. You may hear someone say, "**Do you copy me**? I have **bubble trouble**."

mike — microphone
rig — CB radio
Do you copy me? — Do you hear me?
bubble trouble — tire trouble

Most CB **raddiddios** are in cars, trucks,
houses, or **shaky shanties**. If you carry your
raddiddio when you walk, you have a **stroller**.
A stroller CB has the radio, antenna, and
mike all in one. It runs on its own batteries.

raddiddio — radio
shaky shanty — mobile home
stroller — walkie-talkie radio

You can be a stroller when you have to walk where you're going. A walkie-talkie rig has the mike and speaker close together. You hold it close to your ear and mouth. You can say, "**10-4**," if another good buddy asks you to **eyeball**.

10-4 — yes
eyeball — meet face to face

The CB radio band is divided into 40 channels. With the band divided into 40 channels, more CBers can **holler** without getting walked on. If one channel is crowded with jaw jackers, you can **QSY**.

holler — call on CB radio
QSY — change to another channel

12

When you're ready to **get out**, pick a channel. You can say, "**Break-one-nine**." Buddies listening on channel 19 will hear you. If a good buddy **reads** you on your channel you might hear, "This is Desert Fox. What's your **handle**?"

get out — send out a signal
break-one-nine — I want to talk on channel 19.
read — hear
handle — CB nickname

Sometimes CBers talk about **Smokey**. It may be **Smokey On Two Wheels**, or **Smokey With Ears**. Sometimes Smokey **monitors channel 9** in case a citizen needs help.

Smokey — police
Smokey On Two Wheels — motorcycle officer
Smokey With Ears — police with CB radio
monitor — listen
channel 9 — CB emergency channel

Some CBers **put the hammer down** and **break the double nickel**. One good buddy may say, "The **boulevard is clean**." But even with a clean boulevard, most good buddies don't want to be **roger rollerskates**.

put the hammer down — accelerate, go faster
break the double nickel — go over 55 miles per hour
boulevard is clean — no police in sight
roger rollerskate — fast car

A good buddy may be an **alligator**. Is a buddy who smiles a lot called an alligator? **Negatory**. An alligator is all mouth and no ears. An alligator could even be a **ratchet jaw**.

alligator — CBer who talks too much
negatory — no
ratchet jaw — non-stop talker

16

    If you don't talk too much, you're not an alligator or a ratchet jaw. But you'll have to **walk the dog** and call **port** if you try to run your **Cowboy Cadillac** on **sailboat fuel**.

walk the dog — operate a CB radio
port — home
Cowboy Cadillac — fancy pickup truck
sailboat fuel — out of gas

Lots of good buddies drive **forty-footers**.
If you're a **jockey**, you may have a very clean
K-whopper. That makes you a **big rigger**.

forty-footer — 18-wheeler truck
jockey — someone who drives a truck for a living
K-whopper — Kenworth truck
big rigger — proud driver

Some jockeys drive **bull racks** or **cackle crates**. But if it's yellow with lots of red lights, it's not a bull rack or cackle crate. It's a **winkin' blinkin'**.

bull rack — cattle truck
cackle crate — chicken truck
winkin' blinkin' — school bus

The **Cornbinder** is another popular truck for CB road jockeys. If someone asks if your new Cornbinder rides better than an old **kidney buster**, you can say, "That's a **big 10-4**."

Cornbinder — International truck
kidney buster — old, rough-riding truck
big 10-4 — strong yes

CBers may drive **Jimmys** or **Petes**. As they drive, CBers talk about cars and trucks, the weather, or places to **cut some Zs**. People can get a lot of driving help from CB radio unless they have **peanut butter ears**.

Jimmy — General Motors truck
Pete — Peterbilt truck
cut some Zs — get some sleep
peanut butter ears — bad ears that don't listen

A CB **boast toastie** may ask if you **have ears on** and then tell you about a **10-43** in **Tinsel Town**. 10-43 is an important CB **10-code** message.

boast toastie — a CB expert
have ears on — are listening
Tinsel Town — Hollywood, California
10-43 — heavy traffic
10-code — a way of saying things using numbers

10-94 is a Smokey 10-code number.
A 10-94 on the **boulevard** is bad news.
It means some **yo-yos** are **stepping on Smokey's
toes**. The drag strip is the **bodacious** place
for people to 10-94.

10-94 — drag racing
boulevard — main road or highway
yo-yo — person driving illegally
step on Smokey's toes — drive illegally
bodacious — good

If your car is a **rider**, you may miss a lot
of good CB jaw jacking. You may miss a lot
of **threes and nines** or **eighty-eights** from other
good buddies. You may even miss hearing a **13-26**.

rider — small car without an antenna
threes and nines — hellos
eighty-eights — goodbyes
13-26 — Stay back from the mike when you eat garlic.

24

U. S. 1998276

Maybe your car is a **super skate**. If
Smokey In The Sky sees a super skate on the
big slab, someone is going to get a **bear bite**
for sure. And you know what that means.
Time to **feed the bears**.

super skate — very fast car
Smokey In The Sky — police helicopter
big slab — highway
bear bite — speeding ticket
feed the bears — pay a traffic ticket

CB good buddies go everywhere. You'll find good buddies in **Guitar Town**. Or maybe there's a good buddy **hauling post holes** around the **Shaky Side**. Another good buddy may carry a load of post holes from **Shy Town** to **Hotlanta**.

Guitar Town — Nashville, Tennessee
hauling post holes — driving an empty truck
Shaky Side — California
Shy Town — Chicago, Illinois
Hotlanta — Atlanta, Georgia

If you're not on the Shaky Side, you
may be driving a **bedbug hauler** into **Bean
Town**. And on your way to Bean Town,
you'll have to stop at the **piggy bank**
to toss in a little **lettuce**.

bedbug hauler — furniture moving van
Bean Town — Boston, Massachusetts
piggy bank — toll booth
lettuce — money

You might want to have a special CB handle. If you have good eyes, call yourself The Hawk. Then you can **shake the trees** or **rake the leaves** in a **convoy**.

shake the trees — watch for trouble at the front of a convoy
rake the leaves — watch for trouble at the back of a convoy
convoy — group of vehicles traveling together

Sometimes a handle tells about a good buddy's work. The handle may be **diesel doctor**, **lady in the shoe**, or **draggin' waggin' driver**. But you don't want to be a **turkey**, and only one person in the country can be **First Momma**.

diesel doctor — truck mechanic
lady in the shoe — kindergarten teacher
draggin' waggin' driver — tow truck driver
turkey — bad driver
First Momma — the President's wife; first lady

CBers have handles and **call signs**. Your call sign is a set of letters and numbers. They're yours and no one else can use them.

call sign — letters and numbers for private CB radio, assigned by government

Use your call sign when you start to holler.
And use your call sign when you tell a good
buddy to **truck 'em easy**. It's time to **10-3**.

truck 'em easy — goodbye; good luck
10-3 — turn off the radio

Where to find CB words